CW00553742

how my body works

breathing

Joan Gowenlock

Wayland

how my body works

Breathing
Eating
Growing
Moving
Sleeping
Staying Healthy

Editor: Anna Girling
Designer: Jean Wheeler

First published in 1992 by
Wayland (Publishers) Ltd
61 Western Road, Hove
East Sussex BN3 1JD, England

British Library Cataloguing in Publication Data
Gowenlock, Joan
Breathing.—(How my body works)
I. Title   II. Series
612.21

ISBN 0 7502 0361 7

Typeset by Dorchester Typesetting Group Ltd
Printed and bound in Belgium by Casterman S.A.

All words printed in **bold** are explained in the glossary.

Contents

What do I breathe?

You breathe in air. Air is all around you.

Can you smell it?

Can you see it?

Can you taste it?

Can you
hear it?

Can you feel it?

Why do I breathe?

What goes into your body to keep you alive? You breathe in air and you eat food.

You eat most of your food at meal times. But you are breathing air all the time. You know when you need food because you feel hungry. But you breathe without having to think about it.

Your body uses the air and food to give you **energy**. You need energy for everything you do.

Some things you choose to do, like running around. What do you like doing? Some things you cannot choose to do. Your body does them anyway.

How does air get inside me?

Air comes into your body through your nose and mouth. Hairs in your nose catch some of the dirt and germs in the air. The air is also warmed up.

8

The air goes down the throat and into the windpipe. The windpipe is also called the **trachea**. It looks a bit like the hose on a vacuum cleaner. It leads down to the two lungs.

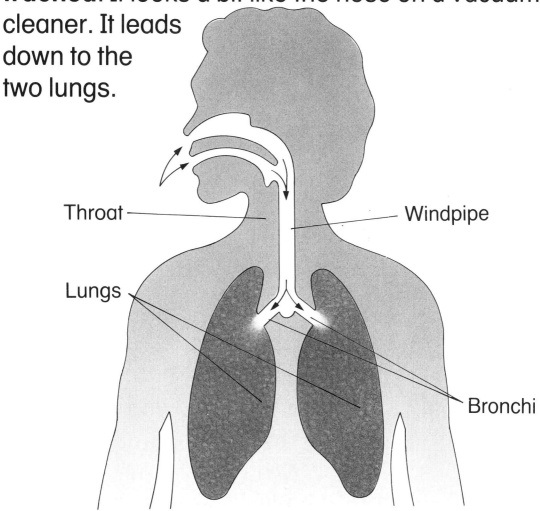

Throat

Windpipe

Lungs

Bronchi

The windpipe divides into two tubes, called bronchi. One goes into each lung.

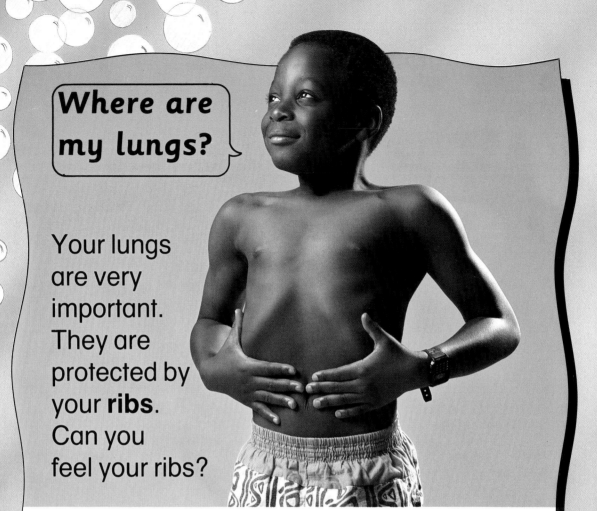

Where are my lungs?

Your lungs are very important. They are protected by your **ribs**. Can you feel your ribs?

Standing quietly, put your hands on the lower part of your ribs. What do you think will happen to your hands when you take a deep breath? What do you see happening? Do your ribs feel any different? What happens when you breathe out again?

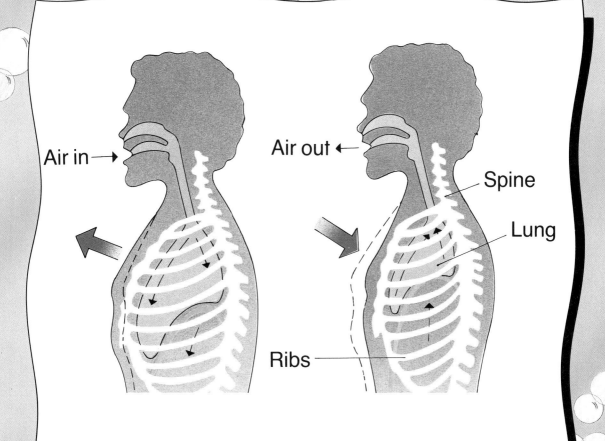

Air in →

Air out ←

Spine

Lung

Ribs

Your lungs are quite big. They take up most of the room under your ribs. When you breathe in air the rib cage gets bigger. When you breathe out it gets smaller.

What happens in my lungs?

Air comes down the bronchi and goes into the lungs. Inside the lungs the tubes start to narrow. They branch into small tubes, like the branches on a tree.

These tubes
get smaller
and smaller
and smaller.

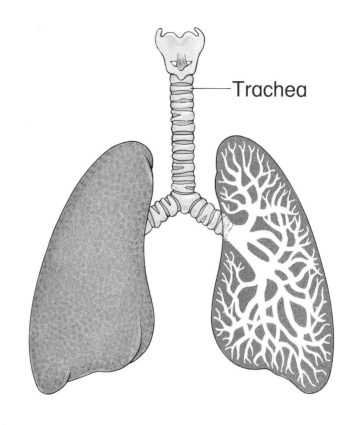

Trachea

At the end of each tube some of the air passes
into the blood. This part of the air is called
oxygen. It is carried by the blood to all parts of
the body.

What do I breathe out?

The body uses some of the oxygen to make energy. At the same time another **gas**, called **carbon dioxide**, is made inside your body.

The carbon dioxide and the extra oxygen are taken by the blood back to the lungs, and then breathed out.

Your lungs are never completely empty. There is always some air left inside them.

Why do we not run out of oxygen?

People and animals all breathe in oxygen and breathe out carbon dioxide to stay alive. Plants take in carbon dioxide and use it to make food in their leaves. As they do this they also make oxygen, which they give out into the air.

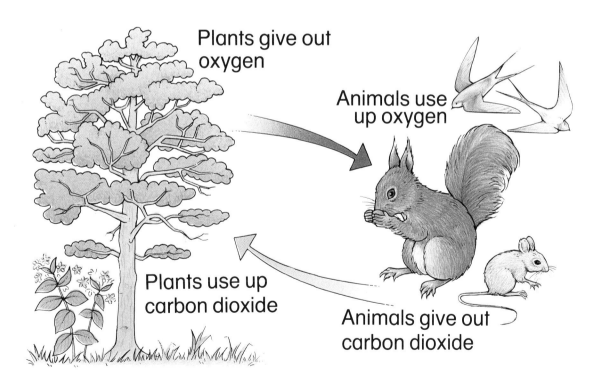

Plants give out oxygen

Animals use up oxygen

Plants use up carbon dioxide

Animals give out carbon dioxide

How do other animals breathe?

All kinds of animals and birds have lungs, just like humans. This big elephant has lungs, and so does the little bird on its back.

Worms breathe through their skin.

16

Dolphins and whales come to the surface of the water to breathe air into their lungs. Can you see this dolphin's blowhole?

Fish have **gills** to take oxygen from the water.

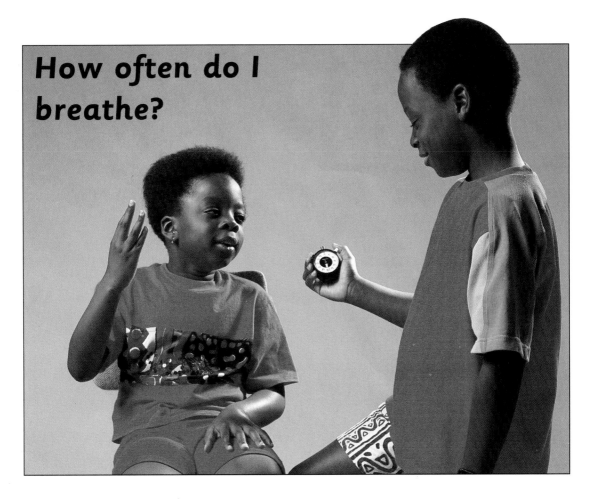

How often do I breathe?

How many times do you think you breathe in and out in one minute?

Ask a friend to help you time your breathing. Sit down quietly. When you are told to start, count the number of breaths you take until your friend tells you to stop at the end of a minute. Were you right with your guess?

What do you think will happen to your breathing if you do some exercise? Try it and time yourself again. Do this with your friends and make a chart to show all your results.

When do you think you breathe most slowly?

What stops food going into my lungs?

Food as well as air is taken into your body through your mouth.

When you have chewed your food, it goes down a tube from your throat to your stomach. This is a different tube from the trachea, which takes air to your lungs.

How does your body know which tube the food should go down?

At the top of the trachea there is a flap, called the epiglottis. When you swallow, the flap covers the top of the trachea to stop the food going into your lungs.

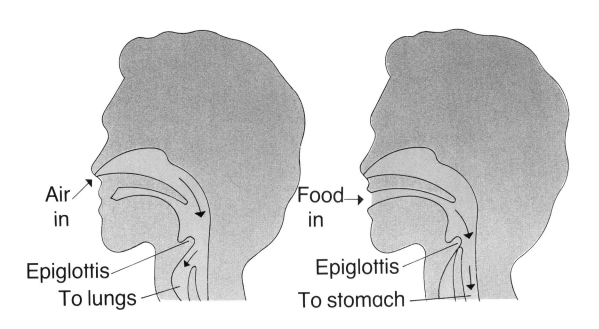

Air in — Epiglottis — To lungs

Food in — Epiglottis — To stomach

What happens if the food starts to go down the wrong tube? Does it make you cough?

What can harm my lungs?

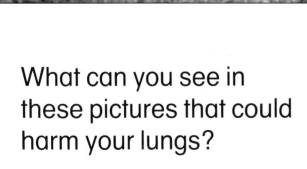

What can you see in these pictures that could harm your lungs?

What did you notice?
How do you think these
things could harm you?

Some people
in the pictures are
wearing masks to
keep safe. What
else could be
done?

What is asthma?

Do you know anyone who has asthma?

Most of the time people who have asthma can breathe easily. But during an asthma attack they find it hard to breathe. They may need to use special **drugs** to help them breathe more easily.

Some young children who have asthma find that it goes away when they grow up.

What is hay fever?

People with hay fever get watery eyes and a runny nose. They sneeze a lot. People get hay fever when there is pollen in the air.

Pollen is a fine dust made by plants in the spring and summer. Look at the pollen falling off these catkins.

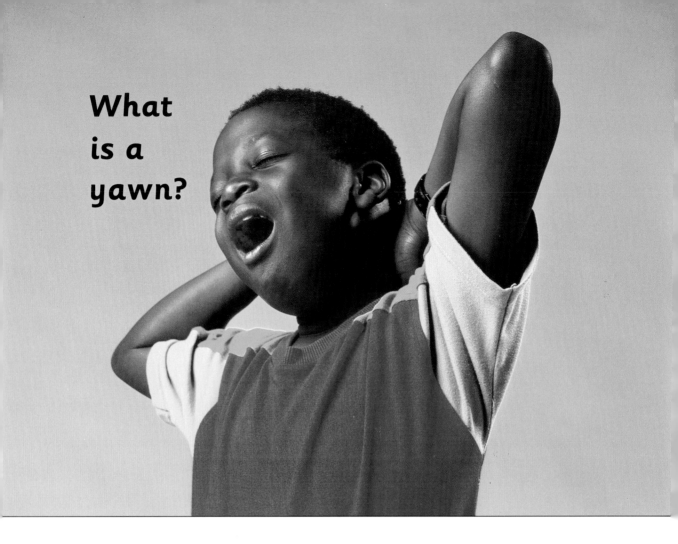

What is a yawn?

A yawn is not made, it just happens. A yawn is when you open your mouth wide and take in a deep breath.

Sometimes you yawn when you are tired or when the room you are in is stuffy.

When you yawn you breathe in extra oxygen. Why do you sometimes need more oxygen?

What is a sneeze?

You sneeze when something tickles the inside of your nose. It is a big breath in and a fast breath out. Why should you use a handkerchief when you sneeze?

In The Guinness Book of Records it says that one person sneezed for 194 days!

Where are we unable to breathe?

You cannot breathe in places where there is not enough air.

If you go underwater for a long time you have to take air with you. How is this diver carrying the air she needs?

In space there is not enough air to breathe. This **astronaut** has to wear a spacesuit with an air supply.

Can you think of any other places where you would need your own air supply?

Glossary

Astronaut Someone who travels in space.

Carbon dioxide A gas made by animals when they breathe.

Drugs Substances that are taken by people when they are ill, to make them better. Some drugs may be harmful.

Energy The ability and strength to move and do things.

Gas Anything that is not solid or liquid, like air.

Gills The parts on each side of a fish which take oxygen from the water.

Oxygen The part of the air you need to breathe to stay alive.

Ribs The bones that make a cage to protect your lungs.

Trachea The tube from the mouth to the lungs.

Books to read

How My Body Works by Althea (Dinosaur, 1989)
Your Body by Caroline Arnold (Ladybird, 1989)
Wheezy by Michael Charlton (Bodley Head, 1988)
Not In Here Dad! by Cheryl Dutton (Arrow, 1990)
Breathing by Joy Richardson (Hodder and
    Stoughton, 1991)

Notes on the National Curriculum

This book is relevant to the following Attainment Targets:

	Level	Statements of Attainment
SCIENCE (Draft Orders October 1991) Attainment Target 1: Scientific investigation		*Pupils should:*
	1	carry out investigations in which they: (a) observe familiar materials and events.
	2	carry out investigations in which they: (a) ask questions such as 'how . . . ?', 'why . . . ?' and 'what will happen if . . . ?', suggest ideas and make predictions. (b) make a series of related observations.
	3	carry out investigations in which they: (b) observe closely and quantify by measuring using appropriate instruments.
Attainment Target 2: Life and living processes	1	(a) be able to name or label the external parts of the human body and the flowering plant. (b) know that there is a wide variety of living things which includes humans.
	2	(a) know that living things need certain conditions to sustain life.
	3	(a) know the basic life processes common to humans and other animals.
MATHEMATICS (Draft Orders October 1991) Attainment Target 1:		*Pupils should:*
	1	(c) make predictions based on experience.
Attainment Target 2:	1	(a) use number in the context of classroom and school.
	3	(e) interpret a range of numbers in the context of measurement or money.
ENGLISH		Children using this book can cover many aspects of the *Reading*, *Speaking* and *Listening* sections of the English National Curriculum.

Index

Picture acknowledgements

The publishers would like to thank the following: Heather Angel 17 top; Chapel Studios 5 bottom right, 27; Bruce Coleman Limited 16 top (H. Reinhard), 16 bottom (A. Davies); Eye Ubiquitous 8 (Y. Nikiteas), 19 (B. Mazzer), 23 bottom (P. Seheult); Frank Lane Picture Agency 23 top (B. Borrell), 25 (A Hamblin); PHOTRI 22 bottom, 29; Tony Stone Worldwide 4 top (C. Bossu-Pica), 28 (C. Harvey); Topham 12; Wayland Picture Library 5 top (A. Blackburn), 6 (T. Hill), 10 (A. Blackburn), 14 (A. Blackburn), 18 (A. Blackburn), 20 (Z. Mukhida), 24 (A. Blackburn), 26 (A. Blackburn); Timothy Woodcock 7; Zefa 4 bottom (Lintham), 5 bottom left (Benser), 17 bottom (A. Power), 22 top (Dr Mueller). Artwork on pages 9, 11, 13, 15 and 21 supplied by John Yates. Background artwork on pages 6-7, 10-11, 14 and 19 supplied by Jenny Hughes. 'Longest sneezing' fact on page 27 is from *The Guinness Book of Records 1992*, copyright © Guinness Publishing 1991.